OPPOSITIONS TO A PROMISE

By Dr. DeVay Myatt, Sr.

xulon PRESS

Copyright © 2009 by Dr. DeVay Myatt

Oppositions To A Promise
by Dr. DeVay Myatt

Printed in the United States of America

ISBN 9781615795802

All rights reserved solely by the author. The author guarantees all contents are original and do not infringe upon the legal rights of any other person or work. No part of this book may be reproduced in any form without the permission of the author. The views expressed in this book are not necessarily those of the publisher.

Unless otherwise indicated, Bible quotations are taken from the King James Version of the Bible.

DeVay Myatt Ministries
P.O. Box 702426
Plymouth, MI 48170

www.xulonpress.com

Dedication

To my wife of twenty-one years, Rosemary, who was placed here in the earth to bring me joy! You have not only been with me in marriage, but also in ministry. Thank you for your support and unselfish love. I love you very much and I thank God for you always.

To my children, Ashley and DeVay II, I love you with all my heart and I am very excited about your future. Thank you for sharing your dad with the world.

To my mother, Gladys Claybrooks, thank you for all of your support and prayers. You have been with me from day one of my ministry. Many times just looking out in the crowd and seeing you there, has given me strength. I love you very much. Special thanks to my dad, Odessa Claybrooks, for your example of a disciplined life.

To my brothers, Rev. Tyrome Myatt, Rev. Alvin Claybrooks, Dr. Roderick Claybrooks, and their wives and children; I could not have asked God for a better family. I am so proud of you. Thank you for taking this kingdom-walk with me.

I also dedicate this book to my best friend, who has gone on to her eternal reward, my grandmother, Mary Myatt.

Acknowledgements

To God I give the Glory for the things He has done. I have been walking with God for over twenty-five years and I am still amazed at His hand in my life. This book was birthed out of my own oppositions as well as through twenty-two years of pastoring where I have watched the saints of God in reach of God's blessings and not taking hold of them because of their own personal struggles. I want to express my appreciation and love for my wife, Rosemary, who has supported me from the beginning and makes it easy to fulfill the will of God.

I am so grateful to my church family, Christ Temple Baptist Church, where the people are "Sacrificing to Win," thank you for your loyalty to the vision. To my man of God, pastor and friend, Bishop William H. Murphy, Jr., your trail blazing has given me much hope. To the prophet in my life, Dr. Michael Shakespeare, thank you for your timely insight and words of wisdom.

Forward

John White speaks of an old Chinese writer who talks about two classes of authors. One kind will accumulate data, sort them and draw a conclusion. The other kind, faced with the same data, incorporates them into his or her life, and later is compelled to write by the urgency of a vital experience. He says consequently there will be two kinds of books. The first book has passed only through the writers' intellect; the second is the costly fruit of the writer's pains, struggles and joys. It reflects wisdom tested in life's laboratory. To use John the apostle's expression, it is the word of the writers' testimony.

Dr. DeVay Myatt belongs to the second kind of writer. His writing grows out of living experience rather than academic detachment. Truth is that biblical truths have to be lived before they can truly be understood. Overseer Myatt writes and speaks out of the hurts and pains of his past, which gives him the ability to reach into an anointing that not many men have been able to reach. Therefore, position yourself to not only be enlightened but also to be moved by the spirit and changed by the revelation that is to be revealed out of the heart of the man of God.

Bishop William Murphy Jr.
Senior Pastor, New Mount Moriah International Church

Introduction

Growing up in the City of Detroit, there was much opposition in my life from the very beginning. I was raised in a house with a man (Odessa Claybrooks) who was not my biological father. My perception of him as the enemy came with much resentment.

To make matters worse, I was constantly reminded by family members of the prominence and success of my biological father (Dr. James Allen Caldwell). Somehow, I felt that I had received the short end of the stick.

Many of the conclusions that I had reached were wrong. I believed that there were so many things that I missed out on having and experiencing because my father was not there. My mother could swing a mean baseball bat, you couldn't out run her and you would get tackled if you received the football, but as accommodating as my mother was, she could never be what I longed for. It was thoughts like this that led me to believe that I would always have an inferior life.

In fact, every friend I had growing up was absent of a father in his or her life. It wasn't until much later in my life that I learned that what I had perceived to be opposition, was really a blessing.

I know what you are thinking, but I couldn't call on Jesus, because I didn't know him and I was certain that He did not know me.

I did not know how important it was for me to overcome at the time. How could I have known that God was preparing me to pastor (oversee) a people of whom 60% percent were fatherless?

I remember when I was in grade school, a teacher by the name of Mrs. Harvey, would always say to me as I stood at her desk, "little boy," she would say with her eyes blazing with fire and a voice with a lack of tolerance, "I've got mine, you have to get yours."

I didn't know at the time that she was speaking of a promise. I was not able to decode what she was saying in my immaturity. But in time, I understood that she was telling me not to allow anyone or anything to keep me from receiving what is rightfully mine.

Jesus said, "The thief's purpose is to steal and kill and destroy. My purpose is to give life in all its fullness." --John 10:10 (NLT).

Here we will to explore and expose the oppositions that may exist in your life and introduce you to the ministry of, El Shaddai, the almighty God, the all-sufficient one, our heavenly father, the one who restores.

Just remember that although the word opposition is a reality and suggests a hostile contrary action or condition, the opposition is not greater than the promise. –Hebrew 12:2.

The promise is a legally binding declaration that gives the person to whom it is made a right to expect or to claim it. It is the performance or forbearance of a specific act. The promise is a reason to expect something, its grounds for expectation of success, improvement or excellence. It's a commitment, an engagement, and undertaking. Simply put, it is a vow.

So regardless of what oppositions you face or where you may be in your life, God is committed to your success. He will never leave you nor forsake you.

Let me stop right here to remind you that in Christ Jesus, you are the seed of Abraham and heirs according to the <u>promise</u>!

Oppositions to a Promise

*"[1]And the LORD spake unto Moses, saying, [2]Send thou men, that they may search the land of Canaan, which I give unto the children of Israel: of every tribe of their fathers shall ye send a man, every one a ruler among them. [3]And Moses by the commandment of the LORD sent them from the wilderness of Paran: all those men were heads of the children of Israel. [17]And Moses sent them to spy out the land of Canaan, and said unto them, Get you up this way southward, and go up into the mountain: [18]And see the land, what it is; and the people that dwelleth therein, whether they be strong or weak, few or many; [19]And what the land is that they dwell in, whether it be good or bad; and what cities they be that they dwell in, whether in tents, or in strong holds; [20]And what the land is, whether it be fat or lean, whether there be wood therein, or not. And be ye of good courage, and bring of the fruit of the land. Now the time was the time of the firstripe grapes."
Numbers 13:1-20*

Just as God sent Moses to bring the children of Israel from Egypt to a land of promise, He has also sent me. It is my responsibility to assist you in getting from where you are to where you need to be. Let me establish that no matter where you are in life you will always find opposition to the promises of the Lord. You may be acquainted with the story of how God sent Moses to free the children of Israel. Remember that they had been put in bondage because they were living a life of wholesale sin. In fact, they had become so entangled, so entwined, so messed up in their life that God had just gotten fed up. Because he has not moved on our situation or because he has not punished when we have done wrong, many times we feel that somehow or somewhere God is on vacation and that he will not receive the report that his children have gone astray. So here they are, God spoke to Moses, he spoke to him of a promise, he spoke to him of a land, and he spoke to him of an inheritance. Let me say to you today, that the inheritance of the Lord is your portion. God said to Moses, I want you to go down and tell Pharaoh to let my people go! Moses' reply to God was where do you want them to go? God spoke and said, "I want to take them to a promise." I want to take them to a land that has no restrictions on my blessings. I want to take them to a place in their lives where they can receive the overflow of my anointing. I want to take them to a place in their lives where they can receive the first fruits of the Lord. I want to take them to a place in their lives or in their walk with me where they shall want for nothing, where they shall be established in my favor. God said to Moses, I want to take them to a land that flows with milk and honey. Now, there is a peculiar thing that we need to talk about here, because this particular land was not vacant. It's reasonable to think that if God had something for you, that someone else would not occupy it. It would be reasonable to think that if God had an anointing for your life that nobody else would be operating in it. It seems reasonable that if God wanted you to have it he would just give it to you. With this kind of reasoning you wouldn't have to do anything except walk in it and claim it and it's your. But God doesn't operate in name-it, claim-it ministries. In fact, every promise that God made is conditional. For example,

> *"If my people, which are called by my name, shall humble themselves, and pray, and seek my face, and turn from their wicked ways; then will I hear from heaven, and will forgive their sin, and will heal their land."* II Chronicles 7:14

> *"Bring ye all the tithes into the storehouse, that there may be meat in mine house, and prove me now herewith, saith the LORD of hosts, if I will not open you the windows of heaven, and pour you out a blessing, that there shall not be room enough to receive it. And I will rebuke the devourer for your sakes, and he shall not destroy the fruits of your ground; neither shall your vine cast her fruit before the time in the field, saith the LORD of hosts. And all nations shall call you blessed: for ye shall be a delightsome land, saith the LORD of hosts."* Mal 3:10-12

He said *then*, I'll take care of you, *then* I'll open up the windows of Heaven and pour you out a blessing that there shall not be room enough in your suitcase to carry it. I'm going to take you to a land that flows;

meaning that it has no hindrances. Let me suggest to you today that the land of Canaan, the land of promise, is not necessarily, although it was then, a geographical location. That Canaan is a metaphor for a place in God that can only be accessed by the believer; it is not a land where you can arrive by plane on your own schedule. The land of Canaan is, in fact, a place that flows like the Bible says, with milk and honey, but the provisions are found in God. It is only in this place that:

> *"Eye has not seen, nor ear heard, nor have entered into the heart of man the things which God has prepared for those who love Him. But God has revealed them to us through His Spirit. For the Spirit searches all things, yes, the deep things of God. For what man knows the things of a man except the spirit of the man which is in him? Even so no one knows the things of God except the Spirit of God. Now we have received, not the spirit of the world, but the Spirit who is from God, that we might know the things that have been freely given to us by God." I Cor. 2:9-12 (NKJV)*

When God was speaking to Moses about Canaan, He was referring to a geographical location that was filled with tangible goods. Today, know that God is trying to get your attention. He is trying to take you to an unfamiliar place in Him. Even though you may know Him, there are some places in Him you have not been and He is waiting to fulfill you there. Often times the problem is that we are looking for the provisions in all the wrong places. We are looking for happiness and joy in all the wrong places. We are looking for success, we are looking for the megabucks, we are looking for all we can get, but we are looking in the wrong direction.

When I started writing this book, the thing that blew my mind and certainly will yours, as you read further, is that the Bible lets us know that they had arrived, but they were not in! And it messed me up, I began to wonder how one could arrive and not be in, how one could have and not attain and how one could be at and not in. The Bible lets us know that the people had arrived at the border of the promise land. And you would think that there would be no reason or anything that would hinder them from crossing over;

nothing that would stop them from obtaining the promise of the Lord. They could see the promise from where they were they only needed to enter and take possession. How often have you found yourself in a similar situation? It's so funny, that we can be so close and yet so far away. It's funny that one can be in reaching distance and still not touch it.

> *"And Moses sware on that day, saying, Surely the land whereon thy feet have trodden shall be thine inheritance, and thy children's for ever, because thou hast wholly followed the LORD my God." Joshua 14:9*

Have you ever wondered why there seems to be no opposition until we start the journey? There appears to be no walls and nobody to stop you, until you start. We are great starters. In fact, we have no problem starting. There is nobody that can start like us. Nobody can beat us off the starting line. When we start we flow so eloquently, we are swift, we are fast and we have vision. It is not in our starting that we falter. It is at the first sign of opposition that we waiver, often falling.

The Bible says that they had arrived at the border, not the promise. God had sent them to the promise, they stopped at the border! God sent them to the promise, but they stopped at the point of opposition! They stopped at the point of labor! It was no problem walking around the desert. It was no problem walking around sand dunes. It was no problem going over mountains. It was no problem in the heat of the day. It was no problem in the cool night. But as soon as they came to the Jordan, the Jordan represented an opposition to the promise. They were like so many of us, we can see it, but we are afraid of failure. We can see it, but we are afraid of drowning in our own ideals. We can see it, but we are afraid of failing in our visions and our own foresights. We are afraid no one will accept us this way, so we stay idly by on the other side of what can be, satisfied with just being at the border of the promise and not living in the promise. Who told you that it would be easy? Now is the time that you cross over, your pass pains have prepared you for the work. Just remember you are a promise to someone else. However, you cannot be who they need until you cross over and receive for yourself. You may have to move into confrontational warfare!

Just remember you will not come here again (to this life). Let me inform you that tomorrow is coming whether you stay where you are or move into your promised life. You will be surprised at how many have become so satisfied with living on the border of success. Many have become so relaxed, so lackadaisical on the border, when all the while God never sent them to the border he sent them to the promise. In fact, God did not place you in the Body to sit idly by. God has saved you, so that you may obtain, that you may possess. Regardless of where you are in life, it's just a border of where you can be. And so He brought you out of the world. I must warn you after reading this book you will no longer be able to sit idly by on the border of God's promises, but you will come to the realization that God has something greater for you and you have been chosen by the one who is anointed to choose, God, Jehovah. Do you know the meaning of success? I'll sum it up in one word – GOD! God never allows a man to come to the brink of failure to leave him there. He only allows him to see this place of failure to recognize his grace, mercy and goodness. God has only brought you to the end of yourself, so that he can take you over to the other side. And now you can recognize Him as the God of all sufficiency; the God that supplies all your needs, El-Shaddai.

The bible, says that they had arrived at the border, not at the promise. The border suggests that there is something "in between". Is there something in between you and what God promised you? Is there something that is causing a delay? Is there something that has caused you to backup and think? Don't look at others funny, when you for the last three years, for the last five years, for the last 10, 15, 20 years, have been living on the borders of promise! So you heard that there were giants in the land and yet greater is He that is within you, than he that is in the world. The God in you is bigger than a giant! Borders suggest that there is something that must be crossed in order to arrive. Can you see it? What problems do you need to cross or overcome? What oppositions do you need the greater one which is in you to handle? Just remember, your oppositions are no more than schoolmasters that prepare you for the promise. I believe deep down inside that you know what God said, you know right from wrong, but somehow you have gotten it in your mind, that if you don't cross over then you are not responsible. That if you never take possession of the promise, God is not going to hold you accountable. But I say to you, whether you know it or not, the God who is the righteous judge shall appear and when he does you must give an account of your life. It does not matter if you lived it in the knowledge of it or the ignorance of it. Paul said, if I may paraphrase, that there are enough signs, enough evidence, just in the sky that you would have to know that there is a God. He said that there is enough evidence in just the singing of the birds, enough evidence in the stars in the sky, there is enough evidence for one to know that God does exist.

> *"Because that which may be known of God is manifest in them; for God hath shewed it unto them. For the invisible things of him from the creation of the world are clearly seen, being understood by the things that are made, even his eternal power and Godhead; so that they are without excuse:"*
> Romans 1:19-20

One day I was talking to a group of men and during the course of our conversation I shared with them the first thing that goes once we get saved; the first thing that we forget, and that is who it was that called us. You know that there is a God, because you know that had God not drawn you, you would not be panting for Him. But one day while you were minding you own business, God spoke to you and called you _____ (name). Now, whether it was an audible voice or not you knew who it was. You knew that where you were going and what you were doing, could not bring you into a kingdom promise. You were fine sitting at home watching the football game or washing your car or straighten up your house, you were doing fine doing your own thing, but you heard his voice and you came running. Now, have you ever taken the time to sit down and play that over in your mind, and said to yourself, wow, I really wouldn't be saved had not something drawn me. You knew it wasn't you, because you had no desire for God. And no, it wasn't the person that invited you to church. How many times had you been invited to church before you accepted the invitation that God's voice was connected to? How many times did you hear the call before you answered and yet when you answered, you knew who it was? If you have ever taken the time to think about that, to play it over in your mind, the first thing you would say is that your life is your choice. Again, after we are saved, the first thing we forget is that it was God who chased us.

> *"For I know the thoughts that I think toward you, saith the LORD, thoughts of peace, and not of evil, to give you an expected end." Jeremiah 29:11*

You were preoccupied, with living, working, tolling over things that are fading away right before your eyes. You were working diligently over things that were rotting and deteriorating right under your nose. The first thing we forget is who called us. Now, once you grab a hold of that knowledge and begin to understand that yes, it was God that called you from where you were, when you were paying Him no attention. What did God see in you that made Him stop doing what He was doing to call you? What was so special about you? What could you do for God? What can you give God? And yet, he paused life. You don't believe he paused life? Let me take you back to the day he called you, the day that the sun stopped, because it was as if you didn't have a clue about what was going on in your life. The world had stopped for just a moment and he spoke and he called you and he drew you and he loved you. What others saw as nothing, he called to himself. And yet the first thing we forget is who called us. The reason I have been harping on the call of God and your forgetting who called you is that I want to bring you into the reality of your salvation, which is not just a deliverance from Hell and the power and effects of sin, but a preservation from destruction and deliverance from danger and difficulty. I don't want you chasing promise decoys. Jesus said that, "I have come that you may have life." God called them and said, "I'm going to take you to a land of promise."

Now, a land of promise suggests that this was a word that God had put in motion before the world began. God was in the beginning before the beginning began. The Bible says that God knew you before the foundation of the world. Therefore, God had established our promise before the beginning began and yet, so many of us have become satisfied on the border. The thing that has blown my mind is the fact that God, who knew us before the beginning began, has tolerated us. He has put up with us and our border living. In fact, border living comes with a border mentality. The border mentality always has the idea that I can't do anything greater than what I have done. So we settle down and make a ministry out of it. That's why you have folk going through the motions, trying to be in the presence of God, because they want to recreate what they experienced last week. But you can't recreate God, because God is the creator. That's a border mentality! The Israelites had come out of 400 years of oppression, it seems to me they would be ready to live high on the hog, but they forgot who it was that said, let's go.

Do you remember when Jesus said to his disciples, "let us go over to the other side?" The storm came and beat on the ship; that was opposition to what he had told them to do. The Bible says Jesus was asleep on the bottom of the ship. The waves were playing leapfrog on the deck of the ship. The lightning was playing tic-tac-toe, in the sky. The thunder was roaring. Jesus slept. The disciples were afraid. Why were they scared? Why were they so afraid? They forgot who it was that had told them; let us go to the other side. You will always be fearful when you are operating in the flesh. Jesus said let us go. Now, any time he says, let us go, it suggests to me that he has already made provision in spite of the oppositions. Although we may see the opposition in the way, we don't have to worry. The only thing that opposition should do is pull faith out of us!

> *"No weapon that is formed against thee shall prosper; and every tongue that shall rise against thee in judgment thou shalt condemn. This is the heritage of the servants of the LORD, and their righteousness is of me, saith the LORD."*
> Isaiah 54:17

God is the Bishop of our destiny! Jesus is the Overseer of our promise! And the Holy Spirit will make sure that no weapon will eat up our promise. We cannot live our lives on the border. There are no provisions on the border. At the border they didn't have to pay any taxes so they became comfortable with border living. Border living suggests that there are no responsibilities on our part. It means that we can receive and not give. It's only when we cross over the border that we have to pay the toll. We cannot go over to the other side if we are not willing to pay the toll. Everybody wants something and nobody wants to pay. Did you honestly think that you were just going to step into the promise of God? Did you honestly think you were just going to sit back and enjoy yourself on the fruit of the land? No, you've got to pay! Look at Numbers 13: 1-2,

> "And the LORD spake unto Moses, saying, Send thou men, that they may search the land of Canaan, which I give unto the children of Israel: of every tribe of their fathers shall ye send a man, every one a ruler among them." Numbers 13:1-2

It would be foolish of us to presume that God, who knows all, was not aware that others inhabited the land of promise. In fact, it was by his direction that Moses sent men to spy out the land. It was merely a test; a test of their love, desire and faith in a God that delivered them time and time again. When God is trying to take us over to a promise, he has to know that we are ready. He does not have time for foolishness. Remember we will not come this way again, so why live the Christ-like life just to get a hereafter reward when we can be enjoying all that He has for us now? Our limitations are only to the degree of our love for Him, our desire to please Him, and our faith in Him. If that sounds like you, then like the lady with the issue of blood, press-in and get what you have been praying for. Do you want what God has for you? Okay, then what are you willing to sacrifice to get it? Friends, self, habits, desires! How bad do you want it? Do you remember what you were willing to do or give up for that first car, house, boyfriend/girlfriend, education, then how much more are you willing to give up to lay hold of the promise? Know that God has a timetable that is just for you! Wait on God and stop being so anxious. Don't you know that God knows what's best for you? He knows the right time to give you what he wants to give you? He already knows that some things that he wants to give you, if given out of season, can mess you up. Stop trying to run before God. Stop trying to get ahead of God. If God is for you, then who can be against you!

> *"What shall we then say to these things?*
> *If God be for us, who can be against us?" Romans 8:31*

Know that God is on your side and know that when he says, wait; it does not always mean no! Know that when he says, not now, it does not mean no! Stop gauging yourself against others. Stop pulling out your measuring stick to see where you are and where someone else is. Let me tell you something, one thing that I do know is that whenever God establishes you, you'll be firmly planted. And that kind of living doesn't come overnight. It does not come without its pitfalls. It does not come without its border crossings, but if you have got to have it now, how long will you keep it? How long will you possess it without God? How long? I didn't say you couldn't get it, but I said that you couldn't keep it without Him. God promised them. Are you getting weary? The Bible said that there will come a time where the people will get weary and not want to hear the Word. They will only want to hear what sounds good. The Bible said that the day will come, where they would rather have their ears tickled, than to hear the truth.

> *"For the time will come when they will not endure sound doctrine; but after their own lusts shall they heap to themselves teachers, having itching*

ears; And they shall turn away their ears from the truth, and shall be turned unto fables." II Timothy 4:3-4

And let me say, although the Bible says that day will come, it does not say that it will happen to all. So, I declare that we are not the people that the Bible is referring to!

The people had grown weary in their journey and their faith in God's promise was waning. Remember, God knows what we need. He knew that they needed proof, so God commanded Moses to send men to explore and scout out the land. He wanted them to see that all that they had endured was worth it and that his promises are sure. Are you like the Israelites, in need of proof of God's promises? Needing proof is really a lack of faith in what God said. I must admit that sometimes because we are such a spoiled people, God has to show us before He can give us. Jesus said to Thomas in St. John 20:29, "you only believe because you have seen, but blessed are they who will believe without proof!" But let me say, *push your faith!* Some of you haven't moved, because you are waiting on a sign. There was a city in the Bible in which Jesus did not work miracles and when the disciples ask Jesus, why, he said, "he did not work a miracle in that place because of unbelief." And you're waiting on a sign. God sees your desire for a sign as unbelief. God sees your need for a sign as an unwillingness to obey his voice. But you want proof! Your life is under divine assignment. Jesus said in essence, I don't have time to satisfy your flesh. Your flesh will not come into agreement with the will of God unless the will of God is in agreement with your flesh. I must do the will of Him that sent me, while it is day because night time cometh. You think you have time, don't you? Night time is coming! God may allow you to carry out some of your unbelieving plans, but if we lean to our own understanding it will cause us to take our own path.

The promise is on the other side of the border. But there is also opposition on the other side of the border. However, He said that He would give them the land. Anything that God gives you my brothers; my sisters, you don't have to fight for it. We must stop being jealous of one another. So what, you have been on the job longer than they have? Let me tell you something. Out of all they have, they wish they had what you have, which is peace that can quench fires. God has put His joy in you. The joy of the Lord has become your strength. I was watching a movie called, "Swordfish," and they were robbing this place and they connected bombs to all the hostages. They connected a bomb that had a tether on it and if one of the hostages strayed too far from the tether, they would blow up. There was a group of policeman that tried to save the life of one woman, but she knew if they took her away from the building she would blow up. They caused not only her life to be taken, but many others. What are you saying, Dr. Myatt? When it feels like your life is about to blow up, when it feels like your life is coming apart then you are running too far away from the Father. And if you continue to run, you are going to blow up! The only reason why you haven't exploded at this point is because God has been keeping you. Get your mind off physical explosion and see how you are wrecking your house. Look at how you are wrecking your mother's mind. Look at what you are doing to your fathers. Look at what you've done to your children. You're talking about an explosion, you're talking about the lives that have been wrecked, come back to safety! I know it doesn't look like the most comfortable place to be, but there is safety in Jesus. In fact, whose life have you wrecked this week? Who have you destroyed, with just a word? They were depending on you. They thought that you were walking in righteousness and they looked over and saw you and they couldn't believe it. And so, they concluded, if this is what Christianity is I don't want it. Do you know why you don't see it? Because it's really not an explosion, it's an implosion and people are blowing up from the inside out. Let me tell you something, you do not have to go out like that. To implode means you can be going through something and nobody ever knows. It means that you just keep it all on the inside and all the while you are tore up, destroyed, distraught and messed up. God never meant for your life to be like that. He does not want you to be one that should be teaching the way but still having a need to be taught. It seems that when others are at a point where they ought to be able to depend on you, you have need that one teaches you again. How is it that we never graduate from the fundamentals of Christianity? It's because we have been content with border living and God never told you to go to the border, he said promise land. Because you have made it this far in this book you can cross over now in Jesus' name. Jesus said, "I am the way!"

There are many amongst us who have accepted Jesus, the Christ, as the living God and yet there is still a remnant of unbelief. Some one can be born again believing God for salvation but they cannot believe God to heal. Isn't that something? I think that one of the most hideous sins that a believer can commit is to harbor unbelief.

So the Bible lets us know, that they sent out twelve spies to see whether the people who dwelled there were strong or weak, few or many; whether the cities were camps or strongholds; whether the land was fat or lean. In other words, they went to see if God's promise was true. They brought back what we call, a majority-minority report. Ten of them, the Bible says, gave a report. They said we must admit that the land is just like God said it was; but we just can't go over there because there are giants dwelling in the land, the walls were tall and they lived in castles. In other words, they saw opposition to what God had promised. Now you have to understand that these giants were in fact, giants in deed for they were the sons of Anak. As a matter of fact, do you recall a fellow by the name of Goliath? The Bible said that Goliath wore a suit of armor that weighed 196 pounds. When we believe that we are able to overcome giants or anything that stands in the way of the promise, then and only then can we obtain the promise. Many of us have not received what God has promised us, because we are afraid of giants. Call your giants what they are. Call your giants out and recognize your giants for what they are. What is your giant? Is it fear? Is it doubt? Is he procrastination? What is your giant? Is it your past? Is it an addiction? Call it out! Do you resent the absence of a parent or maybe it is a sickness? Call him out! It is because of the giants in our lives that we have stopped our progression.

After the spies had completed their search of the land from the wilderness of Zin to Reboh at the entrance of Hamath, they returned saying "surely it flows with milk and honey." Isn't that just what God had promised them? What they had not bargained for was the opposition to that promise. They reported that the people living there were strong giants and the cities fortified. They saw themselves as grasshoppers compared to them and did not believe that they could go against them. Just that quickly they had forgotten that God had promised the land to them and that his promises were sure.

This is what you need to know. God has a way of allowing your enemies to maintain what belongs to you. I know you have driven by that house a couple of times and there was no for sale sign in the yard and someone was living there, they had their car parked in the driveway, but God is just allowing them to maintain your promise. I know you looked over and somebody was driving your car. Come on don't act like you have never said "that's my car." You were riding along and they pulled up along side of you, and you looked over and said "that's my car." God is just allowing them to maintain it. But you have a problem possessing what belongs to you, because there's a giant in that house, there's a giant driving that car, sitting in that executive office or that building that's to be the start of your new business. There are some giants in the land, but God said you can have it! You must stop sitting back waiting for somebody to give you something. Believers have no business in welfare lines, trying to get extra handouts for where you have lack of patience, for where you have lack of faith, for where you have lack of belief. You have no business trusting in the world's system.

> *"And from the days of John the Baptist until now the kingdom of heaven suffereth violence, and the violent take it by force." Matthew 11:12*

God is saying I'll be to you what you want me to be. But you can't receive your portion, because you are trusting in man.

> *"The earth is the LORD's, and the fullness thereof; the world, and they that dwell therein." Psalms 24:1*

Because you fail to take what is yours, you decided to trust in a system that puts you in bondage. Because you fail to trust God, you have to lean to your own understanding. You have to trust in something that is designed to fail you. You see, unbelief, carnality, worldliness, selfishness is no more than giants. How in the world can you follow God with a worldly mentality? Unholiness will only cause your problems to grow. What you have to understand here, is that God has given you your promise, but you are so scared of the giants, that you can't move from the perimeters in which you feel safe. Look at you in your safety zone wishing you could have the promise. Look at you in your safety zone wondering why everybody is moving ahead. Patting yourself on the back and saying how you live holy, praising about the righteous life you claim to live, but snubbing at that person down the street, rehearsing how they don't attend church, but look at them! In verses 28-30 we can see the report of the spies. Verse 28 reads,

> *"Nevertheless the people be strong that dwell in the land, and the cities are walled, and very great: and moreover we saw the children of Anak there. The Amalekites dwell in the land of the south: and the Hittites, and the Jebusites, and the Amorites, dwell in the mountains: and the Canaanites dwell by the sea, and by the coast of Jordan. And Caleb stilled the people before Moses, and said, Let us go up at once, and possess it; for we are well able to overcome it." Numbers 13:28-30*

Now watch this, when I began to look at this, God allowed me insight into what he was doing. I began to see some things here that affected the people. They declare their inability to handle the promise. The majority said, we are not able to go up against the people because they are stronger then we are. And yet the bible said that the children of Israel numbered about 600,000 able men that were well organized. Then they suggested the difficulty of maintaining the possession, because they said, this land has a way of eating up its inhabitants. They manifested the most deplorable and sinful unbelief in forming their conclusion and delivering their report. They totally ignored the presence of God, and totally looked over Jehovah-jireh. When the role call was taken, faith in God was absent and unbelief was present. How in the world, could they forget the Red Sea? You remembered what God did at the Red Sea, when the children of Israel were hemmed up on the other side. How could they forget the cloud by day and fire by night? How could they forget the manna in which God fed them? I know it sounds like I am preaching, so go on and shout, Hallelujah!!!

Remember, that twelve spies went out to scout the land and only ten of them were of the opinion that the opposition to the promise was more than they could handle. The other two spies, Joshua and Caleb, had a different reaction. They believed God! They believed that God was with them and that his promise was sure. They believed that he would bring them to this land and give it to them, no matter what the opposition looked like. They believed that they were well able to inhabit the land and recommended that they should go up at once and possess the land. Notice here that Joshua and Caleb says let us go at once and "possess" it. They do not say, let us go up and "conquer" it. To possess means to take hold. They didn't say lets go "conquer" it, because they knew that the battle was the Lord's and there was nothing to be done, except to enter into what God had promised. Most opposition to God's promises are because of us; how we see things; our unbelief. When God promises it, it's already ours, where we miss it is in taking possession of the promise. How many times have you heard, "the battle is not ours, but the Lord's?" God never told us to fight for the promise. He said possess it!

There are some things God has promised you way back when. But your ways are not God's. Your timing is not God's timing. Pastor, (I hear you saying), I have been trusting God for something, but how long should I wait? And I would say to you, wait until your change comes. You better learn to give God credit. God knows that if he gave you certain things that they would mess you up. There are some things that you just aren't ready for. God has to mature you. God has to get you ready. God has to grow you up. God has to bring you up before he can put you in. There are some things that God wants to give us and they are ours. However, there are some things, if we are honest, whether it's possessions, money or property, if you are honest and think back over your life, if you had received them 5 years ago, it would have destroyed you. If you had received it a little bit sooner you would have messed it up. If you think about it, all of us know someone who never missed anything until they received a car. They would give their last until they got a little money. They would go the last mile of the way before they were given a position.

Let me teach you how to move the hand of God. Keep in mind that this doesn't mean that he will move when you want him to move. God has made us some promises and one such promise is that he would meet our needs. Let me suggest to you that the reason we don't have what we need is because we have not provided God with a need! See, God is not obligated to our wants, he is only obligated to our needs! So when we provide needs God is obligated to meet them. God is true to his word, so when we begin to supply God with needs he begins to meet the demands! Why in the world would God give us money when we don't have a bank account? Why would he give us gas money and we don't have a car? When there is no need, there is no supply! When we paid off the debt we cancelled the need for God to supply. So if we want to move the hand of God, we must learn how to have faith in him. We must learn how to trust him and move out in those areas that the devil said we can't move in. There is nowhere in His word that God promises to take care of our wants. His world clearly tells us to "seek ye first the kingdom of God and his righteousness" and these other things will be given unto us.

Today, I discovered that half of the Christians cannot reach their promise land, simply because of unbelief. Many have told me that I shouldn't expect so much. But if I don't expect it, I won't have it. Touch yourself and say, "if I don't expect it, I won't have it." You can have a package down at the post office, but if you never pick it up you will never possess it. If you were never expecting it, you want look for it. Ten of the spies had their eyes on the giants. But Caleb and Joshua lifted their eyes above their opposition and saw Him that sits on the throne. You see they remembered how easy it was for God to take them across the Red Sea. They remembered how easy it was for God to take them from the hands of Pharaoh. They remembered how easy it was for God to give them water from a rock. Listen, the greatest giant that we have to encounter is our unbelief. Isn't it funny what things we can believe God for and then on the other hand there are things that we just don't believe that God can do for us. I mean he can save our souls, but we don't believe that he can heal our bodies.

There are oppositions to what God has promised you. Right now I feel a shift in the Spirit. And I'm here to declare that it's time for you to face your giants. It's time for you to look your giants in the eye and say to your giants, "God said I can have it"; "God said I can do it." He didn't tell them to go fight, he told them to go take it. God is waiting to do that for you, don't be afraid to face your fears. What are you afraid of? What's stopping you from progressing in life? Why have you been such a long time in the same state, the same predicament? You are still dealing with the same issues, three years later, why? Didn't God tell you, you can overcome this? Didn't God tell you that this wasn't going to kill you? Didn't God tell you he was going to bring you out? Didn't God tell you he was going to sustain you? Didn't God tell you that he was with you? He said, "lo, I'm with you always." Who will stand against what God promised you? He holds the world in his hands. Don't be afraid of the economy. God said I control the economy. Say to yourself, I'm ready to face my giants and trust my God. What are you afraid of? Why are you waiting until tomorrow for what you can do today? Go possess it now!

God does his best work in times of lack. Look what he did with the two fish and five loaves. Look what he did at the widow woman's house. The bible said all she had was enough meal for her and her son to eat and die. God has done some of his best work in times of lack. God does his best work in times of need. Some of you are trying to obligate God and you don't even have a need. You are complaining that you don't have and it's really all because you will not go get it! You are waiting on a better time, you are waiting on a better hour, but now is the acceptable time, now is the time to trust God. Not because you have money in the bank, but because you know God. All the odds are stacked against some of you going to college, but didn't God tell you, he was going to take you there. Didn't God tell you don't worry about the tuition? Who said you can't, you did? Who said you can't do it, you said it? God never said it! Don't blame that on God! Don't tell me that God says you can't prosper, you said that, not God!

Bishop Greg M. Davis, Sr., lists 10 pertinent truths that compliment this book in his Deliverance Now Magazine 2008, Volume 1, Issue 1, and excerpt from his book, "From Promise to Possession," He states we must:

1. **Receive the Promise** – you cannot possess the promise until you receive it! Some of you haven't received His promises. You are having a hard time believing that he can't do what He says He can do. Read the story of Caleb in the book of Joshua and you will see that though it took 40 years, he did receive the promise.

2. **Get Rid of your Egypt Mentality** – you have to get rid of your slavery mentality. If you don't believe that your situation will ever change, then you have to remind yourself that God is not a man who should lie, the devil is a liar.

3. **No more Wandering** – recognize that movement doesn't mean progress. The children of Israel wandered for 40 years. We all know the journey should have taken 14 days but as we read in Deuteronomy they wandered aimlessly looking for the Promised Land.

4. **Possessors Don't Murmur and Complain** – we can't be like the children of Israel and have the spirit of murmuring and complaining.

5. **You Can't Possess until you Receive in your Spirit what has been Promised** – we must believe that God will do what he said. The word tells us that we must "believe in the Lord God, so shall ye be established; believe his prophets, so shall ye prosper – 2 Chronicles 20:20.

6. **You will have to go Against the Crowd in Order to Possess** – you must be delivered from the court of public opinion. The opinion you care about is the one that God has of you. Caleb went against the crowd in Numbers 12:3 and possessed the land. He didn't care what the crowd spoke, he knew what he believed.

7. **You Will Have to Change your Talk in Order to Possess** – you must live in the "now" and not in the "past." Possessors aren't hindered by reports of friends and family. They remain focused. Mark 11:24 tells us we shall have whatsoever we say!

8. **Possessors Are Not Slack** – know that "Slack Brings Lack"! A lazy and slothful person will always operate in lack. Proverbs 10:4 states, "He becometh poor dealeth (with) a slack hand; but the hand of the diligent maketh rich.

9. **Possessors Don't Become Satisfied** – you must understand there is always more! We learn in Numbers 13–14 that Caleb never stopped wanting what God promised him. We are to stand on the same promises! We should

50

declare that it is a season of perpetual blessings. Continuous!

10. **Possessors Seize the Day** – what is your confession of faith? Are you a possessor who seizes moments, or one who seizes days? We know that Jesus did! He seized the day when he dared to not only go to the cross and lay his life down, but be bold enough to get up from the grave.

The one thing I do know and understand about God is that whatever God says we can have, it is ours, but it comes at a price. So the question is not whether or not God can deliver, but the question is, are we willing to face your opposition? The promise is sure, but are we willing to go through in order to obtain? It's funny that we live in a time where no one wants to suffer. No one wants to experience hardships. We feel that it is alright to travel through life on a bed of roses and I suggest to you that traveling on a bed of roses is just as dangerous as traveling on a bed of circumstances. Because one thing that we have to remember about roses is that they have thorns.

You see Christianity may be different things to different minds. Christianity is different things for different individuals. For some people Christianity is only a safety net, a place of refuge. Christianity for some folks is only an escape from hell. Christianity for others has become a relationship with the heavenly Father. So, Christianity presents itself to different people in different forms and you need to arrest yourselves if your version of Christianity is perverted by your wants and your needs. Some inquirers will only see what we can't do. Some inquirers can only see the giants, the tall walls and the big castles that hinder one from entering into the promise land. Maybe you know somebody like that. No matter what happens in life, they can only see the bad side of it. I've shared with many people and I find myself even sharing with you, a young lady once asked me, how I was doing and I responded by saying, no complaints. She said, you won't complain. I assured her that it wasn't because I didn't have any complaints. I simply don't because I realize that although I might have a reason, I don't have a right. God has been good to me! Hasn't he made a way for you? So while we might have a reason, we don't have a right. When you look around, that's all you have to do, is look around yourself. Come out of self and look around and you will begin to see just how blessed you really are. Though you may not have much, there are some that envy what you have. Maybe you have a house with no furniture, but there's somebody that doesn't have a house. We're complaining about the wrong things. You have to learn to find joy and happiness in the little things. In spite of your circumstances there is a reason and a cause to rejoice in the Lord. You have to see that in spite of what you are facing in this life, you can still count on God.

Not long ago we experienced an attack on America, a most profound tragedy and yet in it God has shown up. We saw America showing her true colors. A nation that was founded on Christianity, has now found itself calling upon the God that it had abandoned, so God is winning now! In spite of how it may have looked in New York and in spite of how many lives have been lost, look how many lives have been won! I do not downplay what has happened, but we must learn how to find the good within the bad. That's what will keep us moving, that's what will keep our minds focused and hold our attention and our allegiance. When we know that in all the rubbish, there is hope. We saw people digging folk out of the rubbish on September 11th; this was not a new thing. When I looked at the word of God and when I researched the scriptures, I discovered that when man sinned against a holy God that the world was bombed with Satan's attacks to the point that all of mankind was in rubbish. The world was under sin. So Jesus came along and he began to dig amongst the rubbish. And when he dug amongst the rubbish, that's where he found me! Yes he did! He found me in the ruins of sin. I don't know where he found you. I don't know where you were hanging out at that time, but I was messed up. I was deep below the pile. Where were you? Maybe you were doing pretty good, but living in rubbish. Had cars and houses, but living in rubbish. Sin is rubbish! Maybe you have diamonds and pearls, but are living in rubbish. Jesus, the Son of God, can come along and pulled you out of all of your rubbish. Maybe you are reading this book and need to be freed? Need to be delivered? Pulled out of your mess, pulled out of your dilemmas, pulled out of your circumstances, he's still searching among the ruins and he's not going to give up. Just stick your hand up, so he can see you! But those of us that hold back by reason of difficulties will come to a miserable end. All the spies, when they came back to the camp, confessed that there was something good about the land, but held back in taking possession because of opposition. In Numbers 14, we see that the reluctance of the people to possess the promise provoked God. They were not willing to trust him, even after all that he had previously done. And it was because of this unbelief that God would not let them live to see the promise.

Some of you have shown the spirit of Joshua and Caleb. So I ask today, what is your testimony? It's a land that flows with milk and honey. Listen to that, a land that is able to supply all of your needs. That's the milk, but the honey takes care of your wants. There is no nutritional value in honey. Honey is just the extra! So we see that the land flowed with the need of the milk; because the need meets all of those things in your life that are vital for living. But the honey is that sweet extra stuff that God gives to those that love him. When I read that this land flowed with milk and honey, the thing that stood out in my mind is that true disciples of the Lord Jesus Christ, not weekend want-to-bees, are expected to show the world some natural proof of your heavenly country. What I'm saying is that God wants you to have in this life. He wants you to obtain the best that you can, because he wants to make sure that you have proof, to show a dying world. They came back with grapes as proof that Canaan existed. Now I know what Paul said, "eyes haven't seen, nor have ears heard, neither has it entered into the hearts of man, the things which God has prepared for them that love him." But Paul also says, "…that God has revealed them unto us by his Spirit." A whole lot of us are trying to ride on mama's prayers, trying to ride on mama's grace, trying to ride on mama's relationship, but you got to know Him for yourself. You got to get intimate with Him. Intimacy means, in-to-me-see! Shine the light from Heaven down on my soul, search me Lord and if you find anything that's not like you, you are the potter, I am the clay. Work on me, Hallelujah! You have a promised land. Hold on and don't give up. Hold on because a change is going to come.

Now, I'm going to Heaven and I believe you're going too. And I don't know what you expect to see when you arrive, but I want to see the face of Him that sitteth upon the throne. I want to see the triune Jehovah, the glorified Jesus. I want to see the one that has washed us in his blood. I want to see the one who has made us kings and priests to God. I want to see the one that called himself the Lamb of God. This is why we can't give up now. This is why we can't throw in the towel. This is why we must hasten to our inheritance. This is an inheritance that is secured for us by an immutable thing. What is the immutable thing that secures our inheritance? The immutable thing that secures our inheritance is that God cannot lie! That's an immutable truth. Whatever God says, that settles it! You need to research the scriptures to know what God said. By now, you should be able to hear the words, let us go and possess our promise. Go and possess the things that God has promised when he said, that, "I'll be with you." Those very things, those jobs, those promotions, those houses, and healing, don't stop now. Now is not the time to be a coward. Somebody is saying that I don't want to get in debt in a time like this. Let me tell you something people God is in control of this. And now is the time we ought to be investing in the promise, not holding back from the kingdom. God is saying that you can possess it, but the problem with most of us, we are afraid of the opposition. We are listening to the wrong voices. But now you should hear the words, let us go and possess it, for we are well able! Listen, to his voice.

> *"Fear not, little flock; for it is your Father's good pleasure to give you the kingdom." Luke 12:32*

Now is the acceptable time to claim your promise. What is your promise? Have you thought about it lately? Maybe your promise isn't a house or a car. But maybe your promise is recapturing your son that has strayed away or your daughter that has gone astray. Maybe God told you that he would restore your relationship with your mother or your father, and now is the acceptable time to claim your promise. Don't expect for it to just come to you. He says go and possess it, take it! He didn't say fight. There is a difference between fighting and possessing. When he said possess it, he means just walk up to it and take it in Jesus' name. I know that there are giants but Ephesians 6:12 says,

> "But we wrestle not against flesh and blood, but against principalities, against powers, against rulers of the darkness of this world, against spiritual wickedness in high places."

We must learn to see ourselves as God sees us, not how other people perceive us, but as God sees us. How does God view you? Search his word? He views you as sons and daughters, priests and kings, conquerors, overcomers, sons of the most high. We need to do an investigation of God's views and erase mans. It doesn't make a difference as to how you perceive me, it makes a difference how God views me. It doesn't make a difference what they are saying about you on the job. What did Jesus say about you? The bible says He's on the job, right now in Heaven sitting at the right hand of the Father making intercession, sounds like he's working to me. Dr. Frederick Price says in his book entitled *Integrity*, "that your attitude must change, even though your circumstances remain the same." Everything around you is the same, but your attitude must change. And when your attitude changes it will begin to move and force the hand of your circumstances. With circumstances still the same; you must take God at his word. Let us step out on the boardwalk of trust and faith. Let's not crumble under the hand of a nation that doesn't know God.

Oftentimes the desire to prove God's word comes from a spirit of fear and doubt. There is a tendency amongst believers to send others to prove if God's word is true rather than knowing him for ourselves. When we rely on others we cannot be sure that they don't see giants and walls rather than God's promise. God has a way of allowing our enemies to cultivate those things that belongs to us. It appears to me that God understands just how much we can bare. He knows our level of endurance. That's why he is always interested in standing in us, standing for us, going before us and setting the course of life before we ever arrive. The word of God said that after God made man in His own image and likeness, he says to him, subdue and have dominion. This now belongs to us, rule it, conquer it, take control of it, and take hold of it, possess it!

> *"And God said, Let us make man in our image, after our likeness: and let them have dominion over the fish of the sea,*

and over the fowl of the air, and over the cattle, and over all the earth, and over every creeping thing that creepeth upon the earth. So God created man in his own image, in the image of God created he him; male and female created he them. And God blessed them, and God said unto them, Be fruitful, and multiply, and replenish the earth, and subdue it: and have dominion over the fish of the sea, and over the fowl of the air, and over every living thing that moveth upon the earth" Genesis 1:26-28

In Genesis 1:16-28 we see that there was some action on the part of man. Man must do his part in order for God's provisions to click in. Man must step up to the plate before God's provisions start up. So many times, we are waiting for God, when all the while God is waiting on us. You are waiting for God to do that thing for you. You are waiting for God to turn on the lights. You are waiting for God to give you the job, the promotion, the mate in your life, when all the while God is waiting on you. You can't get a job by sitting at home. God is waiting on you to knock, because he said if you knock, he will open. He said if you seek you shall find. He said if you ask it shall be given to you. That's the word of the Lord. So, it involves your participation. The whole plan of God is finite and infinite. It is God and man working together. Jesus came along and sealed this thing when he prayed, "Father make them one as we are one." When you accepted Christ, you became apart of the glorious triune possession, you also became apart of the works of God. What are you saying man of God? I know you never heard it like this, but this is the way he gave it to me. When you became one with him, He said, "I go to prepare a place for you, so that where I am there shall you be also." Now watch this, he went to prepare for you a kingdom and left you down here to work on a kingdom! What you have to know is that heaven is just an extension of a life that has already begun down here on earth. I really don't like to mess anyone up, but some of your bubbles are going to be burst, to think that you are just going to get to heaven and lounge. But, where is heaven? Heaven has no geographical address. Heaven in fact, is in God. So wherever God is, there is heaven. To be in Him and Him in you, is heaven! Some of you are still waiting to get there when you have already arrived. Jesus said, "that the kingdom of God is at hand, "and they still didn't get.

> *"And when he was demanded of the Pharisees, when the kingdom of God should come, he answered them and said, The kingdom of God cometh not with observation: Neither shall they say, Lo here! or, lo there! for, behold, the kingdom of God is within you"* St. Luke 17:20-21
>
> *"For the kingdom of God is not in word, but in power."* I Cor. 4:20

The kingdom of God is walking beside you. The kingdom of God is talking to you. It's the kingdom that is supplying your provisions.

The bible says that the children of Israel were in route to a land of promise. I told you, but I must tell you again. He said that in that land they would find milk and honey. I told you and I must tell you again, because it needs to be impregnated in you to know that the milk is for necessity. The honey is the extra. God is not only concerned about your needs, but he will also take care of some of those desires. In fact, let me warn you so that you don't step out too often in this arena. Some of your desires have been met today, because God wanted you to have what you wanted; not because it was the will of God for you to have it. Some of us are walking in blessings that were never meant for us, but because we wanted it and because he has become our Father, and we have become his children, he has granted us some of your wants.

There is something that God wants to give you today, there is another level, another ministry, another anointing and another height that God wants to take you to. But guess what, we have a problem, because in our pursuit of these promises, there lays opposition. Isn't it funny how easily we give up when there is opposition. Some folk have a way of blaming God, because of opposition. You go for the loan and they turn you down two times and the first thing you say is that it must be God's will that I don't have it. You go to two car lots and they turn you down on both car lots and you say, it must be the will of God, that I don't get the car. No, it's not the will of God that you walk. It's not the will of God that you catch a bus. One of the most foolish things that I have witnessed in my lifetime is someone standing at the bus stop talking on a cell phone. It's not that God has turned you down that we miss the promise, sometimes its simply because our priorities are out of whack. The reason why we don't want to put things in perspective is because we really don't want to face our giants. We really don't want to face the opposition. We hate to be told "no." We hate for folks to deny us. We can't stand people that put us on hold! There are giants to be encountered in our conquest. I must repeat that there are giants in every promise land. Not just yours! In every promise land there is opposition.

God is concerned about how you obtain what you have and some things are not supposed to come easily. Because the easier it is the less you appreciate what God wants to do. That's why those whom God has delivered from the most have the greatest testimony. That's why those whom God has delivered from the most seems to shout the loudest. Seems to dance! You have to sit them down, because they start thinking and reflecting upon the goodness of the Lord. When they begin to reflect upon the goodness of the Lord, they start thinking about the opposition they had to face, but it was God that saw them through and brought them out and then sat their feet on a solid rock. Jesus is His name! It's a lively stone and his name is Jesus! So in every pursuit, there is an opposition. Jesus says in Matthew 16:24, "if any man will come after me, let him deny himself, pick up his cross and follow me." If anyone would come after me, let them deny their will, their desires, their wants and pursuit after me. I have never seen so many cowardly Christians in all of my life. When we were in the world….. we stood against any thing or anyone that opposed us. When we got saved, we became careful. When we were lost we ran down some alleys that some rats wouldn't go down. When we were lost we found ourselves in some homes, some predicaments, even some giants wouldn't go in. But as soon as we got saved, we got careful! God tells us to do something and we have to pray about it! There are some things we don't have any business praying about. Hello somebody! He told you to go to the local hospital to lay hands on the sick, but instead you pray asking him to go down to the hospital and touch their body and the hands of the doctor caring for them. He didn't tell you to call Him up and send Him. He told you to do it, in Jesus' name. Christ is preparing us for self denial. Our promises cannot be obtained without conquering our fears. Anyone who wishes to rise to a position of preeminence must deny himself many pleasures. But if you want to excel, then there are going to have to be some pleasures, some desires that others enjoy that you're going to have to deny yourself the right to enjoy. In order to arrive, some of us may have to stay in the library, stay at the desk, denying ourselves the enjoyment that others participate in. Some pleasures are our opposition.

Some of the giants that are in opposition to our possessing the promise are in us. Let's look at the boxer; he must go into training. The boxer doesn't think in his mind, he's going to get in the ring and knock someone out without ever getting hit. We don't want to get hit! We're walking around talking about if God loves me, he wouldn't let this happen to me. It's happening to us because he loves us! We're going through, because of the love of God. In every pursuit there are perils, before there is a victory. The giants that are in us are in the shape of evil principles, sin, immoral acts and thoughts. These giants must to be conquered! They need to be God handled, not man handled! All giants are not external. Some are internal giants. Fear, doubt, procrastination are some of the biggest giants. The giant of procrastination manifests because we can't believe God said it; we have to go to seven seminars for somebody to confirm, what God has already told us. Why do we need to go and stand in somebody's line for them to tell us, what God has already said? He already told us to come out from amongst them. But we have to stand in somebody's line so they can lay hands on us and say the very same thing that God has already told us. The only difference is they might blow on us! We have to know why God has placed us, where we are. There is no greater joy than to know that we are where we are by divine providence. It truly is something to know that we are walking in the will of God and that he is leading our footsteps. We must see that this is bigger than what it is. It has to be more than just "God led me here". This speaks of our obedience to his voice. And you said you couldn't hear him. You said, he wasn't talking to you, but you're reading this book today, because he compelled you to! But you say when you pray, he doesn't speak to you. Well, it's not that he's not talking; he's just not saying what you want to hear!

We are always able to conquer spiritual adversaries with the help of God. We are always able to win in spite of how life looks, with God all things, not some things, but all things are possible to them that believe. Some Christians don't understand that their greatest gifting is faith. A lot of people think, I have what I have, because I am a pastor. This is not true, in fact, I will suggest to you that my paycheck is smaller than yours. But it's where I put my trust; it's where I place my sights and my faith. My hope is built on Christ, the solid rock, all other ground is sinking sand!

> "Now faith is the substance of things hoped for, the evidence of things not seen. But without faith it is impossible to please him: for he that cometh to God must believe that he is, and that he is a rewarder of them that diligently seek him."
> Hebrews 11:1,6

I don't drive the car I drive, because I have big money. I drive the car I drive, because I have a big God. I don't live in the house I live in because I have big money, I live in the house I live in because I have a big God! I can look out of my back door and see my horses running around. I'm just bragging on my God! The problem is when you learn how to read and write, you started putting a large "S" on Satan in stead of a small "s." You put a big "P" on problem in stead of a small "p," capitalizing upon your circumstances. My circumstances and the world's circumstances, does not dictate to my God. Be in a recession if you want to. But I live by faith, not by sight. I can't depend on what I see. I want you to step out into this world that was pre-fashioned for you to rule and speak to it. Now open you mouth and tell this world that you know it was made for you to conquer!

> *"And God said, Let us make man in our image, after our likeness: and let them have dominion over the fish of the sea, and over the fowl of the air, and over the cattle, and over all the earth, and over every creeping thing that creepeth upon the earth. So God created man in his own image, in the image of God created he him; male and female created he them***.*** *And God blessed them, and God said unto them, Be fruitful, and multiply, and replenish the earth, and subdue it: and have dominion over the fish of the sea, and over the fowl of the air, and over every living thing that moveth upon the earth." Genesis 1:26-28*

This world knows how to move at your voice. I know you've tried to call things that are not as though they were and this world rebelled. Inside yourself you fight and struggle to follow the will of God and you must! I tell you my beloved; it is not hard to live a Christian life. The only reason why you are struggling is because you have not made up your mind. The only reason why you have problems walking this walk is because you are not willing to talk the talk. The only reason why you are not prospering in this land is because you are not willing to deny your flesh. If you attempt great things, you're going to have to trust him. You cannot expect to do anything great without him. Did you know that there is a point that is beyond recovery? I don't know who said it, but it bears repeating, "they who will not, when they can, shall not when they will." Now you take that and chew on it, because I would have to write a whole new book to explain! I'm saying that you can get so complacent and so satisfied living a faithless life, that you no longer even have a will or a desire; you are beyond the point of recovery!

The report from the scouts affirmed that the land flowed with milk and honey; that the promise of God was true. And yet, they were fearful of the inhabitants of the land because they perceived them to be more powerful than the God that had shown himself faithful to them over and over again. This cowardice attitude resulted in 600,000 of them dying in the wilderness. They had enough sense and courage to start out for the promise, but they didn't have enough faith and trust to finish. We cannot allow fear, to keep us from God's promises for our lives. II Timothy 1:7 reminds us, "For God hath not given us the spirit of fear; but of power, and of love, and of a sound mind."

So what are we building our hopes on? How big is your giant really and how long has he been harassing you? He must be brought to the surface. He must be exposed. You never can get help from your problem if you never acknowledge that you have a problem. What is your giant? How long has he been hindering you? How long has he been destroying your marriage? How long has he been running up and down in your affairs? He must be exposed! He must be brought to the surface! You must stop protecting him! God has not destroyed the fears in our lives, because we have been protecting them. We have wrapped ourselves in a cocoon; thinking that we are going to come out someday as a beautiful butterfly, but that's a lie! He must be exposed! I don't care how deep you wrap up in your self-made security blanket; it will never bring you to the point of victory. You may be having problems with your spouse, because you have an argumentative spirit and if you never expose him, if you never say I have an argumentative spirit, he will invite other giants. And when they come, they will come bigger and better.

Make today the last time that you are harassed by your giants. Today is the day of your restoration! If you believe that, I want you to begin to think through your life. And I want you to begin to look at these giants for who they really are. And I want you to expose them, bring them to the surface and into captivity. How do you bring them to captivity? You bring them into captivity by acknowledging that they have no place in your life.

About the Author

Overseer, Dr. DeVay Myatt, Sr., started his ministry under the tutelage of Dr. J. Allen Caldwell, Pastor of the Burnette Missionary Baptist Church in Detroit, Michigan, over 26 years ago. In 1987, at the young age of 25, he was appointed as the Pastor of the Christ Temple Missionary Baptist Church, Detroit, Michigan, where he has served faithfully for the past 22 years.

Overseer, Dr. DeVay Myatt Sr., is a multi-talented young man in his own right. God has gifted him in the areas of healing, teaching, preaching, administration, singing and song writing, using these gifts to spread the word of God. His travels have taken him abroad. He has traveled extensively for eight years to Andros Island, Bahamas and Freeport, Bahamas for missionary work, witnessing, preaching, teaching and evangelizing. He has conducted many revivals, seminars and counseling sessions. Many souls have been saved during these missions. His travels, also has taken him to Garmish, Germany for three weeks, ministering to our own US Army troops serving their needs.

He serves as the CEO, of DeVay Myatt Ministries, on the Board of Directors for the Family Life Center in Pontiac, Michigan, and as Overseer of the Southern District - Full Gospel Church Fellowship in Detroit, Michigan, where there is a strong sense of God, the Church and Family.

He has received esteem recognition from Mayor Kwame M. Kilpatrick, Governor Jennifer M. Granholm and President George W. Bush, for his outstanding servitude.

He also received an Honorary Doctorate Degree of Divinity Degree from Saint Thomas Christian College, Jacksonville, Florida, January 2007, from President, Dr. Zamekio Jackson.

Overseer, Dr. DeVay Myatt, Sr. is married to his beautiful wife, Rosemary G. Myatt. They have been married for 21 years and the proud parents of two spirit-filled and gifted children, Ashley and DeVay II.

God is truly working in his life.

Available Books by Dr. DeVay Myatt

The work of those that serve at the altar during the worship and prayer experience is handled in many ways. In his manual, *Prayer Counselor*, Dr. Myatt addresses proper protocol and brings clarity and definition to the role and responsibilities of those assigned/appointed to assist those who come to the altar seeking prayer.

For those who preside over the altar as well as those who serve at the altar, *Prayer Counselor* is a valuable tool with practical application and guiding principles that will enhance their ability to serve more effectively and efficiently.

Order Form

Name: _____

Address: _____

City: _____

State: _____   Zip: _____

Email: _____

Telephone: _____

Check One: ☐ Check ☐ Debit ☐ Credit Card ☐ Paypal

Name on Card: _____

Card #: _____

Exp. Date: _____   SEC CODE: _____

Cachet: _____ Quantity $ _____

DeVay Myatt Ministries
P.O. Box 702426
Plymouth, MI 48170
Phone: (313) 770-7143
Fax: (313) 934-4340

Email: dmyatt@devaymyattministries.org